ILEANA GONZALEZ MONSERRAT

HAVANA 1995
ENGLISH VERSION

The uprising of the Cuban people in July 11, 2021
gave hope for freedom in the Island

Copyright © 2025 by Ileana Gonzalez Monserrat

All rights reserved. No part of this publication may be reproduced, distributed, or transmitted in any form or by any means, including, photocopying,recording, or other electronic or mechanical methods, without the prior written permission of the copyright owner and the publisher, except in the case of brief quotations embodied in critical reviews and certain other noncommercial uses permitted by copyright law. For permission requests, write to the publisher, addressed "Attention: Permissions Coordinator," at the address below.

ARPress
45 Dan Road Suite 5
Canton MA 02021
Hotline: 1(888) 821-0229
Fax: 1(508) 545-7580

Ordering Information:
Quantity sales. Special discounts are available on quantity purchases by corporations, associations, and others. For details, contact the publisher at the address above.

Printed in the United States of America.

ISBN-13:   Softcover   979-8-89676-536-3
                  eBook   979-8-89676-537-0

Library of Congress Control Number: 2024926679

The book cover features the Capitol of Havana, a landmark commissioned by Cuban President Gerardo Machado and constructed between 1926 and 1929.

Table of Contents

Foreword To The First Edition. I

Foreword To The Second Edition. III

Foreword To The Third Edition. IV

Chapter One 1

Chapter Two 8

Chapter Three 11

Chapter Four 15

Chapter Five 18

Chapter Six 22

Chapter Seven 24

Chapter Eight 28

Chapter Nine 32

Chapter Ten 35

Chapter Eleven 39

Chapter Twelve 42

Chapter Thirteen 46

Chapter Fourteen 50

Epilogue 52

To the island of my birth.

"I live in Cuba. I have always lived in Cuba. Those years of wandering the world that they have talked so much about, are my lies, my falsifications because I have always lived in Cuba."

Heberto Padilla «Out of the Game», 1971

- But what is oppression?

-It consists of avoiding the spontaneous manifestation of the other person, or his own expression, it is to curtail freedom.

Reinaldo Arenas

«Memories and Presence», Ediciones Universal

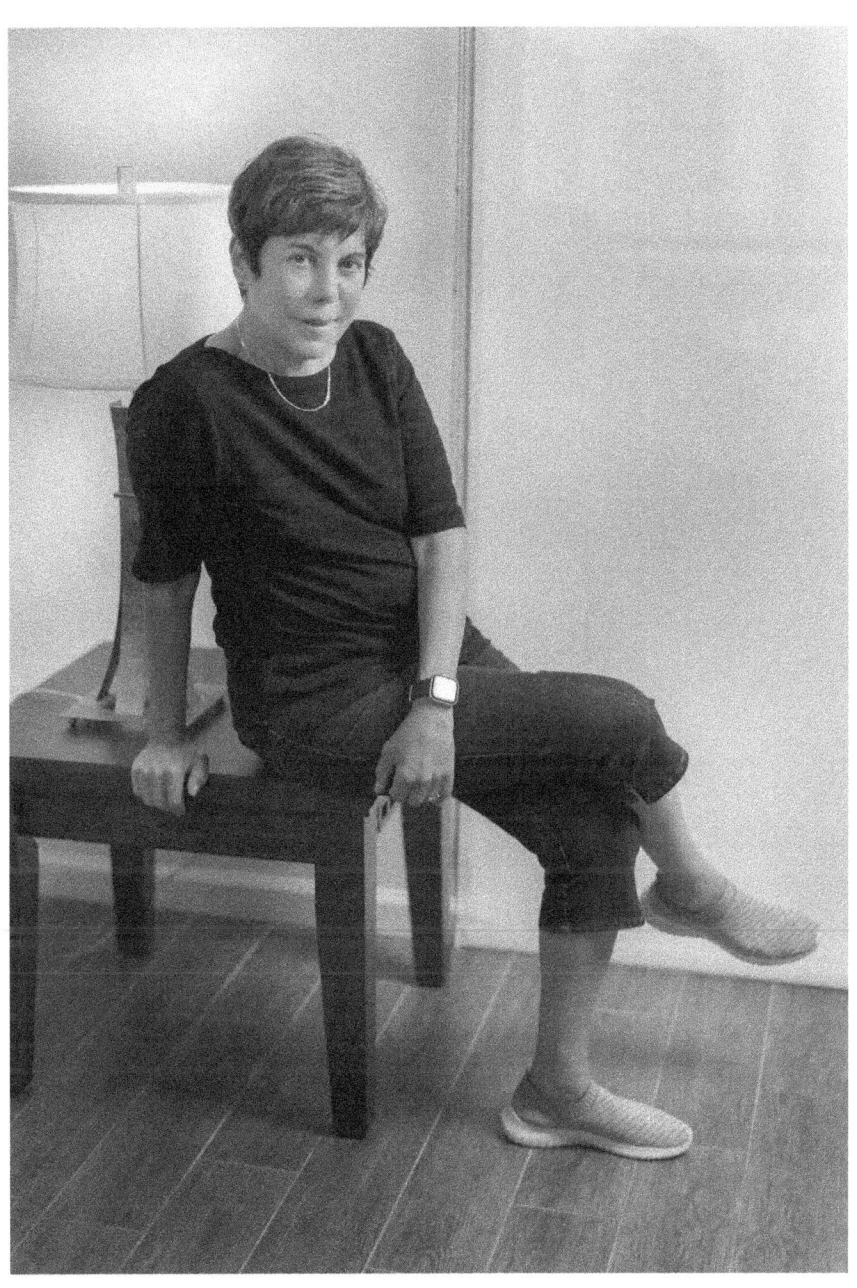

Photography: Julio C. Rodriguez

FOREWORD TO THE FIRST EDITION.

"It is really pleasing, when you leave the homeland to find a homeland in the land of others."

José Marti

I've written about a dream. A dream that must materialize. A dream that was asleep and is now rushing to come through. Freedom needs to come for all Cubans as it moves through the world.
When I started writing this story not even the Berlin Wall had been torn down. It was in early October 1989. A week later, the most unexpected political changes of our time began occurring. Then I felt afraid of my vision. But, encouraged by my colleagues in the office (Americans not knowing in depth the problematic nature of Cuba), I decided to continue with the idea. Thus appeared a draft that spoke of the freedom of Cuba as something tangible, describing the encounter between two individuals: one in Castro's Cuba, the other in exile. The story is narrated by the one who returns from the United States, explaining his conflicts in a lyrical way despite his pragmatic upbringing. Cuba's freedom confronts him with a lost identity that he now wants to regain. He meets his country, the disaster, the reconstruction and Vladimir, his companion made of illusions or perhaps of his new realities.
They live, vibrate, and cry the dream. There is fear of waking up but continuing to dream also hurts. Everything is immersed in a landscape that is muddled with reality and something that can happen at any time: the return. That old question that has changed its route so many times. I know there will be many returns, because even those who ignore the homeland even out of curiosity will return. Therefore, in these pages there is more agony than joy; more than the encounter with the past there is an encounter with us.

And there is a little bit of every Cuban in these writings and a little bit of each of any other. Because I have written for everyone who wants to recover their past. For any immigrant who feels the need to look back.

I have written for everyone who is alienated or lost in other places. I have written for those who have faith in the future and in change, and for anyone who wants to mourn for Cuba or know of the joy of our people.

And most of all, I have written for Cuba. For that yesterday that was stolen from her, for her presence that we long for and for that dream that it found on the Malecon -the ocean seashore and boardwalk of Havana, the new breeze of the future that we await.

Los Angeles, February 1990.

FOREWORD TO THE SECOND EDITION.

On November 9, 1989, an event occurred that shocked the world: the Berlin Wall fell. With this came the collapse of the Soviet Union and most of the countries that made up the socialist bloc. I had hoped that freedom would also come to Cuba. Already before, and almost as an omen, I began the idea of a draft that projected the freedom of the island.

Then, with the illusion of the new era and the countries' liberation in 1991, the work was published within few weeks. I was reflecting then on all these years of socialism on the island. The identity of the Cubans had been lacerated, creating an exile and new generations of Cubans scattered around the world. I took as a reference the year 1995 representing anytime when Cuba might be free.

At the meeting of two men, now freed and separated by history, there was talk of rebuilding the island. Everything in the book happens within the parameters of a dream of one of the protagonists.

Today in the course of 2021 the idea of freedom remains uncertain after 62 years of totalitarianism. Fidel Castro died leaving the infrastructure, the personal and national identity totally forged. Raúl Castro, his brother assigned to power, has withdrawn from the scene, transferring power to Miguel Díaz-Canel.

Cuba today is a living museum of the failure of the revolution and socialism. Despite all the time that has passed Havana, 1995 continues to be the dream of all Cubans, regardless of any transformation, personal or collective adaptation.

Today, on a visit to Miami from Los Angeles, I was surprised by an unprecedented event. On July11, Cuba stood up crying out for an end to tyranny. During the following days demonstrations of support for our brothers and sisters have been unleashed on the island and all over the world with the motto of Patria y Vida, defying that of Patria o Muerte.

Ileana González Monserrat Miami, July 17, 2021

FOREWORD TO THE THIRD EDITION.

This is the third edition of the book. When AR approached me to republish it, I was initially reluctant. After much consideration, I agreed, postponing the process until after my return from a trip to Asia so that I could be available. At the time, I didn't realize how much my travels would enhance or even reshape my perspective on this work, originally published more than 35 years ago.

In the first edition, I had hoped that Cuba's freedom would emerge as part of the Soviet Union's collapse. But nothing happened. The years passed, and the country continued its disintegration.

In July 2021, the Cuban people's uprising reignited a glimmer of hope within me. Yet, the hope was quickly overshadowed by severe human rights violations, and to this day, many innocent individuals remain imprisoned.

In this edition, I reflected on my visit to Singapore with such a strong economy and many notable features. I couldn't help to make a comparison between Cuba and Singapore—two small islands seemingly alike in size and population, yet whose path diverged into sparkly contrasting realities. Their stories offer a powerful lens through which to understand the transformative power of leadership, governance, and human determination.

Singapore is a marvel of ingenuity. With no oil, no fertile lands, and no abundance of minerals, it seemed destined for obscurity. Yet, through visionary governance, a relentless focus on education, and disciplined economic policies, it transformed itself into a global hub of trade, technology, and finance. Its people, empowered by access to world-class education and opportunities, fostered a culture of resilience and creativity. Open markets, meritocracy, and a vision of sustainability elevated the island to international prominence—a shining example of how human ingenuity can overcome natural limitations.

Cuba, in contrast, was once blessed with abundant natural resources: fertile soil, a warm climate perfect for agriculture, and rich deposits of minerals. However, decades of mismanagement under a socialist regime have left it a shadow of its former self. Centralized control stifled innovation and ambition, while inefficiency and corruption became deeply entrenched. Infrastructure crumbled, and once-thriving industries withered. After 65 years of dictatorship, the very essence of Cuba's national identity has eroded. The Cuban people, rich in spirit but poor in opportunity, now endure under the weight of oppression and diminishing hope under socialism. Cuban dictatorship blames the U.S. embargo for the island's suffering, but the real chains are internal. Farmers are forbidden from farming freely, fishermen can't fish without state control, and independent thought is criminalized. The regime uses the embargo as a scapegoat to mask its failures, justify repression, and avoid reform. This is the way to deflect responsibility, justify repression, control the economy, maintain the ideological narrative, and avoid reform.

The most alarming consequence of this prolonged dictatorship, however, is the visible and profound disintegration of the Cuban people—physically, emotionally, and socially. Years ago, the people's collective desire for freedom was palpable; they aspired to reclaim their nation and their future. Today, that determination has been replaced by a survival mode, a stark reflection of the toll taken by decades of deprivation and repression. The vibrant spirit of a people once unified in hope has fractured under the weight of hopelessness.

This human disintegration is Cuba's greatest tragedy. It is a silent erosion, more devastating than the collapse of its infrastructure or economy. Rebuilding Cuba will require more than political or economic reform—it demands a rekindling of the Cuban people's sense of identity, purpose, and hope. Now, more than ever, Cuba needs help—from the international community, from its diaspora, and from all who believe in the resilience of the human spirit.

The stark difference between the two islands underscores the consequences of governance. On Singapore, economic openness and political pragmatism created a society where growth and opportunity flourish. In Cuba, idealistic but rigid policies led to stagnation, poverty, and the tragic squandering of natural and human potential.

Today, Cuba stands at a crossroads. After decades of isolation and systemic decay, the nation's recovery may require external support—whether through partnerships with other countries or the solidarity of those millions in exile. The path forward demands not just resources but a reawakening of its people's determination to rebuild their identity and their future.

The juxtaposition of Singapore and Cuba is a poignant reminder that success is not merely a product of natural wealth. It stems from visionary leadership, freedom, and the ability to adapt. As I reflect on Cuba's journey and the struggles of its people, I remain hopeful that, with the right support and determination, the island can rediscover its lost potential and redefine its destiny.

Singapore, October 2024

Remains of the Berlin Wall for history where the author wrote.

"Berlin 1989"

"La Habana 1995"

CHAPTER ONE

The day is fading away and with it my long journey. Sleep overcomes me and so, slowly, as it must be dying, I am reaching another dimension, the one that has no distance and where the present, the past and the future have the same form.

I feel somewhat incoherent, but the tropical breeze refreshes my consciousness. An awareness marked by the bitterness of being an exile but also a consciousness enriched by the years of achievements and efforts.

However, now my reflections became unnecessary, what did it matter if I was back on the Island now.

It had rained in the morning and in these hours of the afternoon a soft rainbow adorned the Havana Malecon[1]. This seashore is not just any seashore, or any wall or the boundary between land and sea. No, this seashore is like a century-old hero, a great giant who has a memory, a story to tell. He not only gives contour to the capital but is unique and legendary. Over the years he has told the waves our secrets: sad history of abuses, of betrayals, of corrupt governments. And it seems as if the sea is enraged and there is an eternal rumble behind it. It is the thunder of its waves.

When I lived far from Cuba and I remembered the Malecon, its image came in unison with the sound of the waves. And my memory smelled of the sea, with a taste of salt and pain of time. This is the true image of this Havana's significant boardwalk. It is a painting that has melody. It is something simple that refreshes our soul. Although it separates the sea from the land, it is like a starting point and like the return itself. He was an imaginary separation between Cubans here and there.

---

1 Havana Malecon. The Malecon is a 5-mile-long promenade in Havana that runs along the coast.

This symbol was kept with us during all our struggles since colonial times. The Cubans of exile, those of here, those of there, the brave, the tasteless, the usual ones.

How many years have passed! From a single type of Cuban evolved many different ones. The big questions are: will we now achieve a true republic? Will we have learned over all these years the basic elements of a democracy adaptable to our conditions? Will it be possible to reach a future between all Cubans forged abroad and those who forged themselves in communism? Will Cuban poets return, those who have had to sing in someone else's land? Will the peasants who worked on other horizons come? Will the children who forgot their language come? Will this be Martí's dream once and for all?

Will we all wake up together once and for all?

And so, with my lonely thoughts, I began to look at Havana from my inert space. And I began to cry with joy, with pain, with fear, with courage. My longing fulfilled: I was back in my country. I had stopped I do not know for how long. I was drowning in my own emotions. I looked around and a couple sitting on the wall adorning the Coast of Havana. They were like the couples of other years, or maybe they were the same, because nothing had happened. My reality was the one that changed, not that of others.

The voice of the manicero[2] surprised me. I felt electricity in my veins. Everything remained the same, everything was seen up close. I stopped in front of one of the couples. They did not perceive me. They looked at each other slowly as if they wanted to recreate an old memory .

I was so confused, I wanted to know what year I was in, because I did not dare to ask. I continued my walk, I wanted to escape from myself. Now running I crossed the street and entered the city. Then, I raised my eyes and saw a sign: Happy New Year 1996!

There was not any joy for it being a holiday. The buildings were unpainted and dirty. They looked musty and sorry for their attire. There were hardly any people on the streets. Haven't they all come

---

[2] Havana's street peanut vendor.

back from Miami? I thought. And the others? Where are the ones here, the ones who never left?

The sweat on my forehead betrayed my restlessness. It was the only evidence of the tropical heat. Then I knew that I existed, that I was detained in a space in the Caribbean where joy had dissolved in the Cold War that was left behind. The desolation hurts my eyes. I wanted to go back to something I did not know; maybe to the comfortable freedom of the world I came from, maybe to the peace of waiting for what was happening to me in this moment. A slim woman, composed, with a certain European air approached me. Is she Cuban, I asked myself, maybe she will tell me who I am?

"Madam, do you know where we are, who are we, are you Cuban?".

The figure disappeared. Perplexed, I started running again. I crossed many streets; I do not know how many. I was galloping the streets of Havana with daring.

Everything was completely deserted. There was no new return or old shelter. thought of the couple on the boardwalk and changed course to return to the Malecon wall. Not far away I spotted a taxi. It was a 1951 Chevrolet. To my astonishment it was entirely new. Then I remembered the sign: Happy New Year 1996!

"Have I read 1956?"

Then, a voice brought me out of my stupefaction. An almost familiar, exclusive, resoundingly Cuban accent asked me:

"Are you from the community?"[3]

The voice seemed strange or coming from another time. "The...the community?"

I sounded like my own echo. Maybe it was my conscience. "Yes, that, of course, I'm from the community"

There, in front of me, a car, a man and thousands of questions. And so, with instant familiarity, I jumped into the car. I indicated that I

---

[3] Exiled Cubans who visited the island for the first time after more than twenty years with a special permit were called "the community."

wanted to go around the city for about an hour. (How sad it was to see represented in an hour the destruction of a beautiful city!)

I was ashamed that I could not state any of the names of the streets. Maybe I never knew those names. The individual agreed. Neither of us stipulated price. It seemed as if it was not necessary. It was not necessary.

The car began to roll out through the sad and dormant streets. I carried the hum of the Malecon inside my heart. There were no words, just thoughts of return. For a while I returned to my confused consciousness and got lost in the silence and pain of the encounter.

Some soft music came from the radio. The music was languid and seemed to have forgotten the tropical edge because the sadness of the destruction. There was a fulminant interruption on the radio and Castro's words were heard: «Fatherland or death, we will win!... Patria o Muerte, Venceremos!"

And even louder and more intolerable: "Fatherland or death, we will win!"

"Don't panic," he assured me, "we heard it so that it would not be forgotten. We cannot forget that. It is always going to be that way, by the time we are gone the generations to come will not be able to forget it either. Do not be afraid, Cuba is free, it is free now.

There was silence, perfect, no hurry. Everything was strange and new. The man enjoyed his freedom. I still did not feel it. Then, a single question appeared. We both interrupted almost in unison:

"You are?" "Your name?"

The coincidence gave us confidence. We smiled. Our identity became necessary, almost imminent. "My name is Vladimir."

He warmly extended his hand to me going over the front seat. I was surprised by his name. He noticed my amazement; he felt my astonishment. That name was a transplant from the other side of the planet. It sounded like an occupation. This was my first encounter with the Island, and... this name made me see Cuba now so close and still so far away. I was already realizing that, although I had returned, I had been left behind, in a time, where the dynamics of the years were not part of my return.

"Vladimir? Vladimir?" —I repeated slowly. "Yes, my name is Vladimir." And so, I heard from a Cuban voice the memories of a red age.

I readjusted back into the seat to be in line with my new circumstances. I indicated to him, almost as if justifying it, as if I wanted to defend him from the evidence of history, that his name was not very Cuban, that he was Soviet, that it was an implant, that it was a transplant of the lie ...

"Mine is Juan. Well..., John, my name is John."

"John, John? "His voice sounded energetic and ironic. " Your name is very American, sir."

The voice rumbled raw without disguising his bitterness, his disdain, his despotism. Would John be the other side of the other lie? It was interesting, my defendant was now acting as a prosecutor. The stranger and I, doubly distant, looked like enemies of a time. We were the enemies of time.

"You know, my name is Vladimir, because the legit one, or the one I did not know, was forbidden to me by the Russians, the last occupants of the island.

He spoke and gesticulated with that special arrogance of every Cuban. He did not seem arrogant. He was arrogant!

"My parents knew how to survive in their time. Everyone is born in their own time. I had no choice. You did."

There was silence. We breathe together the reminder of a of wounded Cuba. Each time the sound of the sea became more distant. Now we could only hear 'reproaches' of a fulminant encounter with the new era and the past.

"Yes, it's true, I had an alternative, but its name was "banishment." The exile that was never seen in the colorful photos, an exile cold, despotic, irreconcilable. Yes, it is true, I had freedom of movement, of expression, of those silent expressions, because you cannot love the country that gave your life in exile. You stop being you. To become an amalgam of many others, an incoherent mass that believe they are free. The free ones who are imprisoned in the green prisons of the dollars and the consumerism… And I suffered, silently, my sentimentality, my nostalgia."

Vladimir listened attentively, his apparent contempt beginning to show signs of understanding.

"I was like an illegitimate son, an outsider in another's house. I wanted to adapt, but I felt a distance. There was a distance. So, I accepted my condition. I learned to look at it all from afar. That is how they look at the foreigners. That is how they look at us. And with my sensitivity always alert, and my best eloquence, the eloquence of an exile, I lived as they all live, without a homeland and pretending with a smile. And… And now, I do not feel this present, because the past programmed me differently and now, I feel that way: different, that is how I feel, a foreigner in my own land.

These are the wounds produced by time and an exile. Still here… here… Back to what is mine, I do not think I belong. I breathe and feel the emptiness of the years I was away. That may be what I will be. That is who I am: a foreigner in any system."

I did not want to continue because I was drowning in all the damage done to my identity. But I continued talking. Vladimir was attentive. It is good that the transplanted ones are heard!

"They never forgive us," I said, "There was no longer anguish in my voice, perhaps it was resignation. "The ones here will feel that way because we left; and we, because they stayed. We will all have reasons. No one will win this battle. We think differently and after all we are the same. A latent result of a people's war against themselves."

Vladimir was silent. There was no discord. You could not hear anything anymore, not Vladimir, not the waves, not myself. Maybe we were forgiving ourselves. The man in front of the seat looked like a repentant child. There was no need for a dialogue. Everything was a product of foreign forces, greater than us. There was the urgency, the need to exchange experiences from another perspective, that of the future of

Cuba. From that future that gives birth to the "new era", the time of now. Cuba is now free and faces two refugees in search of a dissolved time... And so, this meeting was a concrete synthesis of two characters forged in strange lands: Castro's Cuba, my world of the North...

CHAPTER TWO

The car was still going slow. There was only one stranger and me and a beginning. Two Cuban representatives of different time, although parallel, that converged on the same question: the uncertain future of a country with sores. I wondered if they actually believed what was happening. We were scared.

For the exiled, Cuba was an island with a past alone; for the survivor of communism, Cuba was only an instant space with no past, present, or future. The need to survive absorbed everything.

"In the freedom of Cuba there was never faith," I dared to say, "only a distance dream, sometimes closer than ever, but always becoming unreachable."

I remember that in the United States for me the present and future of Cuba had dissolved. This was the end of our only recount. Expressions always referred to something that had been. Everything was in the past tense. We were past. The 'present' was also the 'now' in the past. And so, many new years became old. Many new eras made stages... The world revolved around us. And we, those here, those over there, remained static in the uncertain wait. And over the years the "wait" had already forgotten us.

So, unknowingly, I sold my values to the American. I was not even asked to do so. I lived between two different idiosyncrasies and needed to solve that disjunctive. And when the time of total adaptation came, I gave up, I was exhausted from the battle, a battle where the enemy was everything that was not myself. My name took on a new concept, the concept of change.

I was upset to the point where I changed my mannerisms, and everything was from the North. My mannerisms said it all. My accent was polished so as not to sound like an immigrant. Already assimilated and perfect I had entered the jungle of the exiled, of the unpatriotic ones, of the transported. Everything was done, my concrete convictions were the convictions of the dollar.

My god! One day I woke up from my lethargy and saw my accomplishments in front of a mirror full of gray hair. Then an inner force, a prosecutor imprisoning my psyche called me a "coward" and I ventured into my new comeback. I wanted to go back to myself and find my roots. I no longer wanted to beg for a homeland, or belonging, I no longer wanted to recognize what I did not have, I no longer wanted to be out of place with a happy smile. And I began to become wiser.

I asked and inquired about what had been buried. The sleeping island, the one that woke up today next to all of us and what I heard tasted bitter to me: a story full of abuses, of a brutal Spain, Yankee humiliations, Russian totalitarianism. Nobody understood me. Returning from a farewell had some mysteries. The Cubans themselves spoke of Cuba always as the same usual. I felt like a foreigner among those in the North, and worst of all, a foreigner among mine. The Cubans saw me from a distance, I was not the same and neither were they. Who was I and who were they? The only thing we agreed on was wanting Cuba's freedom. Now we began to understand each other. Just freedom for the wandering island. That island that has begged century after century for freedom and justice.

About this no one spoke with common sense or seriousness. It was only part of an everyday event and not something that could really come. I do not blame them. Time had erased the patriotism of the early years. There was no sincerity. The consumerism, and everyday life sort of erase all feelings of loyalty to the cause of Cuba. Others, the most loyal, always followed the cause. Now I was just an adapted entity with no homeland and no flag.

I was so frustrated that I returned to what was easiest, to what I knew well: the way of the Americans. We do not return only physically but also with the soul and the heart. And I physically returned to the North, but I left my soul and my heart here, where I breathe now and live the legendary dream of all of us. But even with the hurt, I regrouped my soul and heart back and I took everything from Cuba, I thought I had completely detached myself; it was, I thought, a perfect transplant. We adapt to the environment so as not to perish. It is that need for affiliation that leads us to commit. After all, I had tried. I decided to forget about my family, my friends, the dead ones in Cuba... And so, many years passed, and they brought a family, a career, some children... And a second departure.

CHAPTER THREE

Suddenly and without knowing why, I could not speak. This great encounter was now entering another territory of my exile, my ambivalence towards the United States. I then tried to search in the baggage of my memory for all the difficult events of my life, which would impress Vladimir, all those things I experienced in the 'imperialist monster'. (I thought with a Castroist intonation, I think ironically, we have all transformed ourselves a bit, damn Castro language). I will speak like this to Vladimir, «the seed»[4] his consciousness will be tied to Moscow for a long time, perhaps forever. In the meantime, I hope he forgave me. However, the 'imperialist monster' was vanishing from my story, I did not find those horrible facts that I had experience there.

And looking at every possible event, I didn't find anything of such magnitude. There was no alternative but to accept that those of who were able to transform ourselves into other entities were at least free, and the rigor of communism only came to us by correspondence. The escapees are not heroes.

Now exhausted, with my suitcase empty, the Malecon far away and freedom in front of me, I felt satisfied, and I lowered my forehead. I felt like a monster myself, I lived my own tragedy. After all, what could I really say about a country that opened the doors to me when my doors were closed, and what could I say about some more or less light things? Perhaps my perception, my values, my language, my social stratum, my race had changed, which, with the description of being Hispanic, without even realizing it, now belonged to an agglomerated invention with dimensions to control me. Maybe much more than the others, quite a bit more. After all, these qualifiers are nothing more than the intrigues of the Anglo-Saxon separatists, they live these divisions and

---

4   "The seed" Analogy with propaganda and constant political indoctrination. The Cuban who developed in socialism is said to carry "the seed."

suffer them as well. They are free at times too. But anyway, when you come from a slave land, the differences are nothing. So, in this social catalog I was a Hispanic -American. That was my price, all dissolved in those two words. But, what else does it give, this became insignificant in the face of the remoteness of Cuba. When I justified that the Anglo-Saxon was insolent and ignorant, I was comforted by the wait, then all my prejudices became temporary. Sometimes I was ashamed to see them all as adversaries, "they gave you freedom"; my conscience rescued me. Then I felt shame, the shame of the immigrant, of the tramp, of the 'desterrado', the guilt of the ungrateful. I was simply ungrateful.

"Yes, Vladimir," I said, "I think after all I didn't do badly. I was a free wanderer."

This was said with some irony. I do not know if he perceived it. I didn't know what I felt: hatred, gratitude, indifference, admiration? But I have to forgive, we are all very confused.

After all, I had used the same opportunities as the native. I arrived last and ventured with the others. But why do I feel that way? Do I feel the grudge of the illegitimate? What really weighed on me? Was it my resentment that had been heard without listening but not heard? Or was it the sense of sentimentalism that I inherited from the torn Iberia peninsula?

After all, maybe Cuba's history was not different from that of any other country. Society was tolerant of my adversity. That was it, no more and no less. And I just wanted a political audience. A hearing that felt my sorrow, when in my own confusion I was not even sure of having it. No, sorry, I was not crucified. And now I was alone, empty-handed. In my main role, my autobiography was imperceptible. Perhaps the simplest Cubans, who did not stop to reflect, were always the best. They left Cuba; new challenges hurt them little. They lived better.

When it was allowed to do so, they returned and visited the island, and without washing their hands and souls greeted the military fighter, the lady of Comite[5] So cheerful and without guilt, they danced to the sound of the music that was being played in the port of Mariel(6).

---

5 El Comite de Defensa de la Revolución. founded on September 28, 1960 in Havana, with the purpose of surveillance of the population. Such comites were created in every block of every neighborhood to coerce the citizens.

It was an embarrassment, but they were going to bring the relatives. There was music in the Mariel and thousands of dead at sea... And perhaps these Cubans honored Cuba more than I did. Without so many worries, without falsehood, they adapted. They learned to sail in the difficult waters of the Americans. And then we all danced together to the music of the possessions of a car and an air conditioner.

Who would be right? I felt anguished now; next to Vladimir everything had an imaginary nuance. I had time to suffer. Vladimir was only able to survive. His rough hands and sun-tanned body were the best examples of his sad life. I felt ashamed. If in the U.S.A. I felt alienated, my references were more mine than external ones. There in the distance, the true results: "To have been entirely free." Now I was back, and like a slap in my face or ironically an extra dose of freedom; not even now after I had been educated, raised and 'trained' there, not even anyone noticed my life. Nor did they before, they never saw me, nor did they feel me, nor did they perceive me, nor did they find me. Perhaps anonymity is freedom, the only true freedom, where neither entry the exit is charged. I understand. Ungrateful? Maybe, but I'm playing my best card.

I laughed to myself; this was the monologue of my return. I discovered that my drama began on my own stage, that I was empty-handed, my role had not begun. The 'other' audience, the one that never enjoyed the 'monstruo' waits. They have faith in what we learned, but they lack patience. I do not have much time. The case of Cuba was one more in the history of humanity, but the only one in my history. That of having wanted to feel an oppression that rendered my action useless. I wanted to justify my inability to seek the solutions that my country needed. In the meantime, I entertained myself in my role of a misunderstood person, with no audience. Meanwhile, there, those, the busiest, or the others, those simple ones, perhaps the best ones, without hiding in some masks danced in the Mariel[6]; but they conquered their relatives, who had to wait and in another port without music: Camarioca[7]. Those Cubans, where are they? I think they are still there, scattered around

---

6   Between April and October 1980, more than 125,000 Cubans left the island, via the port of Mariel, 30 kilometers from the capital, heading to the United states fleeing the communist regime. More than 100,000 settled in Miami, Florida.

7   15 years before the exodus of Mariel, another group left at the port of Camarioca in Matanzas, between September 28th and November 15 1965. By this way 2,979 Cubans left and another 2,104 remain in Camarioca until they were picked up on ships rented by the United States government and relatives.

the world or in Miami, in their factories, with their gold chains and their promises to conquer something... And they say they are going to come back to Cuba. I do not resent them. In so many ways they are better than me.

Vladimir read my dilemma, my anguish, my confusion, my exile from within.

CHAPTER FOUR

And now Vladimir spoke with solemn parsimony of his boring childhood. His 'Edad de Oro'[8] never shone. He told me that when he was growing up, he wondered where the joy and hope that children should feel went.

And he only had these concerns because the castristas told him about the mambises[9] and their 'Apostol' in a way that he did not understand. His worst dilemma that he was a free child with tied hands. Then, in longing moments, he took refuge in the literature of Jose Marti and saw the big lie discovering that Marti did not agree with the bondage of the soul. These works were like food to a mind strangled by opprobrium. These pages gave hope and joy—which he never knew—to a young man who had a sad childhood, without pencils, without notebooks and without hope.

Thus, he learned sanity and made a name for himself, a communist man on the outside, Marti on the inside. He became a man staying away, that way he could scape from the vulgarity of his environment. He was no longer a young man with a rifle, but a young man with a guide.

Without other references, the palms of the Island took some human virtue and an unpredictable beauty. He then asked his mother why the palm trees of Cuba were so symbolic, and his mother, who was a noble and simple woman, could not answer him. And he looked for the answers in the great, the brave, his best friend, his only teacher: Marti.

Vladimir did not know the other Cuba, the one that smiled, the one that I left. It was not necessary. The one for which the Malecon rumbled, that one, mine; that one, the one that gives one hope; that

---

8   La Edad de Oro written by Jose Marti for children.
9   Mambises. Cuban guerrillas soldiers that fought against Spain for Independence in the The Ten Year's War 1868-1878.

one, with its best white rose[10], he lived it drop by drop with the dreams of José Martí. He composed it in his mind by weaving it with poems and chimeras.

Let us hope that this is the real moment for that Cuba to be thrown at us.

Vladimir said, in a low voice, that in his childhood he played he was a cloud that landed in the distance, and he saw Cuba from above and near and far and his crying was the rain that fell to wash away the filth of his imperfect world.

Now, I could imagine that when they took the boy, with his pioneer[11] costume and his "voluntario" mask, he would surely leave sad and when he was going to the countryside to work land... in his "school to the field"[12] he looked at her so fertile, so rich and at the same time so arid, it already had the cold of Siberia. Poor Cuban land, so humiliated and hurt; he was embarrassed to ask her for fruit. Here he began his exile, his exile in his own homeland, he was banished on his own soil.

But the child was not afraid, he wanted to grow tall, tall, tall, like the palm he always wanted to be, so tall to see what was on the other side. As a child his mother was worried about the things he said, because children his age did not talk like that. He was a pioneer, a pioneer dressed up in uniform, a pioneer of the revolution.

While I was sitting in that back seat, thought how brave and intelligent that young man was. I imagined when the child was in uniform; he did not see much difference between the slaves that Marti spoke and his uniform with the smell of bullets. That is why he appreciated Marti's writings in a unique way. If it had not been for them, he would not have known of his own internal and external slavery.

---

10 White Rose. Known poem by Jose Marti.
11 Pioneer. In 1961, the government targeted children from the 1st grade to the 9th grade to indoctrinate them. They were called pioneers of the revolution and drilled them with the constant repetition, "Pioneers for Communism, we will be like Che."
12 In the 1970s schools were established in the countryside, to alternate study with agricultural work, to contribute to the formation of the "new man" High schools and university students spent 45 days in a camp dedicated solely to the work of the fields. Then, in the 1980s, the days were reduced by establishing February the month to the countryside. As of 2011, these and other similar modalities were disappearing because of inefficiency.

Then I understood that the truth only exists when we compare it to other truths. This saved him. I imagined that this is how Vladimir grew up, simple as his only toy, the "basic"[13]. And still being blind, he saw it all through Marti's vision. His exile was his best escape to the horizon, to the future. Unknowingly he was always big, long, long as his palms trees.

---

13 In the mid-1960s parents were allowed to buy three type of toys for their children "the basic" or expensive one or of better quality, the "non basic" or poor quality and sometimes a third one by a drawing process.

CHAPTER FIVE

"Despite my sacrifice from my own space, I wanted to study and prepare myself, the revolution did not recognize me as it did with others. I struggled with my books alone. Every morning in the light of a quinqué (kerosene lamp) shone the hope of going abroad to make me a better people. In honest moments I wanted to overcome myself so that the revolution would send me out. It was the only way to play progress. I knew of colleagues with destinies in Prague or Warsaw. With these hopes, the vicissitudes of the environment were less arduous. And I dreamed of Prague and Warsaw as did the others, 'the capable ones'. With my full faculties I wanted to be an honor for Cuba; but the revolution did not understand independent minds but bent brains. And my dream of Prague became the horror of Angola[14]. I did not understand anything. After all, I had fulfilled all the requirements of community sacrifice. I knew they distrusted me, that they already knew I was a rebellious young man with a survivor's mask. Then they sent me to the other side of the planet to pay for what Castroism had given me. I had to pay off the debt of being what I never wanted to be. Since I was a child, I was told that everything, absolutely I owed everything to the revolution.

And I spent hours inventorying my own void. Perhaps the reference, most of all, was that of an education that began with the Manifesto and ended in Africa. I believe that everything you receive has a stipulated price. And the cycle of history punishes us in reverse. Everything is the same from afar and up close, the past returns. From Africa they brought the slaves, now Cuba was exporting their own, yes, their own. What an irony! They threw me into a distant place... I did not know

---

[14] The Castro's greatest ambition was to export his revolution to all the countries in the world. An example of this was the its interference in the wars of Africa, such as the Cuban intervention in the Angolan war that lasted more than 13 years. At that time, more than 350,000 Cuban passed through Angola.

when or for how long, or why I was fighting. As an automaton, I lived the anonymity of my dissolved dreams.

Thus, as a passage from a grim vision, Africa became a grave for the Cubans who did not return. Mothers waiting, for the return of their children from this useless war. All in vain. The mothers kept going back home alone to cry. They were tired, but they also needed to continue paying the debt to the fake 'Revolution' imposed on them.

Listening to the story of this new man, I thought about how difficult it was to have lived in such a system, so different from mine.

I do not know if it was harder to have been exiled in another land, or in one's own. I knew him rebellious, growing up with a mercenary beret, to go trumpeting shots in a distant country. It did not matter if it were Angola or Nicaragua, the important thing was to bring the howls of the Sierra Maestra to perpetuate the misery of the miserable.

Also, I realized that time punished Vladimir as well. He became his own enemy when had to open trenches on those foreign grounds. Poor man who only managed to leave Cuba to win honors with blood.

They made him a mercenary and won a medal, his only medal: the medal of repudiation.

I am sure he carried the flag of only one star with shame.

I felt sorry for both of us... for our past. Two men lost in distant dimensions, tempted to drown their faith. He was sent to Africa, I... I had to shoot bullets in Vietnam. War is the same anywhere. Everything tastes like it is biting you. The one who wins it only loses a little less. When I thought about "his war", mine, all my reality exploded in front of my eyes.

How come I did not remember this war? Had I really forgotten it? I was sorry!

To evoke this war was to acknowledge that my youth had been cast in the graves of my dead comrades.

"Now yes," - I said, "now I want you to know something."

Vladimir began to hear me in amazement. I seemed to transform myself into the worst of oneself. Knowing more about this man had finally opened old wounds. It seemed as if we were both competing in a rendezvous of tragedies. But it was necessary to know each other, to make a beginning with the understanding and consciousness of the bitter past of our exiles.

"They took me to a war that was not mine and with other motives I defended an ideal that they gave me in pieces so that my own could be dissolved. I was not a Cuban then, but a Hispanic. A citizen made of pieces that had a repertoire of civilian duties waiting for me in Vietnam."

Vladimir became interested and asked questions. I loved myself, I felt like a hero, I was finally beginning to be heard. He asked judiciously, as if he knew the answers. He knew the answers.

We both relived our wars. Our previous remoteness was now invisible. Since Vladimir wanted to hear more, I continued.

"I went because I had to, the free ones also received orders. I had no choice. My freedom knew of napalm. I had to represent the nation that gave me freedom. I carried the fifty stars, when it would have been easier to carry the solitary one. I was comforted because I was not alone. The 'others', the other victims, those on my side, did not know what they were defending either. Then wounded by the bullets that entered my Cuban flesh, yes, my Cuban, American, Hispanic, indecisive, and smelly body, I was disqualified from the war. I returned to a room of veterans in a hospital with wounds deeper than those of my body. I spent days, hours, months, feeling bursts of bullets and the bullets sounded a thousand ways; at times, they were like the hum of the waves. Again, those waves, perpetual, breaking the Coast of the Malecon habanero and my soul little by little! Here in the hospital, wounded, I also had my own spirit cornered. But at least I was still better than the ones who never came back. Or those who arrived all disfigured."

Vladimir was not breathing; he just heard me. He died slowly, to revive himself over and over with the inner smile of his hope he learned from

Marti. I felt sorry for both of us and the need to hug him. But I did not. It was not possible. We were both strongmen, the guerrillas of the same nightmare. I finally saw my crucifixion!

I already forgave him for his Castro evolution, and he understood my other façade.

"The war is over, and I started mine internal one. It had all been absurd, misguided. For years I felt fear and the horror of loss. On my return I found new needs. All of us victims of opulent systems capable of misaligning our hearts. In short, we both pierced bodies that could have been those of another enemy. In the midst of my confusion, I counted to my astonishment the final answer, my final return. Today I am back in Cuba, but I actually came back from that moment. In the hospital I knew that my place was really in the sleeping island, filled with many "Vladimirs". That island that awaited me while I played an alien Armageddon.

CHAPTER SIX

We kept silent. And we returned to our physical space, our reconciliation with the Havana of the moment. There was moisture in the air and in our eyes. I saw the destruction more than Vladimir. I came from the North. He lived here, further south.

Reconstruction was upon us with the speed of time. Vladimir, Cuba, and I were coming back from the war, from the years, from a time in detention. For the first time since my return, I felt immense joy and I kept quiet. I felt entirely Cuban. Without another qualifier. Did I regain my identity? Which one of them: the one I never lost or the one I never had?

I wanted to get out of the car and spontaneously hug everyone, but there was no one. I was a lonely sailor in an old car that was new, or new without getting old. Is that because I am dreaming or dreaming, I was dreaming?

When did I go crazy, or did I stop dreaming?

Luckily Vladimir was still there, with his worn clothes and tanned body, his communist evolution with Martian flashes. Then I checked that everything was still valid, and I imagined everyone coming back and Miami depopulated. Everyone wanted to live again, to see, to rebuild, to die nowhere else but here… All those Cubans over there are the best hope for our ruined economy.

I was savoring my last comeback. And I only began to see the present and the future.

"This is Virtudes Street. Do you know that? " Vladimir interrupted.

"I remember it; how can I not remember that street! "I said with pride, and I felt my identity again making a return.

"There you see Galiano." "Galiano?"

"Yes, of course, Galiano."

I breathed high and deep to fill my spirit with these streets of mine. Havana and I, we were enjoying our encounter.

CHAPTER SEVEN

It was getting dark, and Havana was even more lonely. In no way had I aspired to find a flourishing Havana, but neither was this loneliness what I had imagined. Infanta no longer looked like a street but a gloomy alley. I once again doubted my reality or played with my fantasy.

But when I least expected it, in the distance, I deciphered a malnourished people who seemed to be waiting for the arrival of the car. People were gathering and there was pain in their faces. Many men had their fists clenched, as if they were going to fight. Across the street, to my astonishment, another group of people began to gather; they looked better dressed; some were smiling and seemed to be happy with our arrival. There was no need to ask what was going on, the two Cubas were going to meet to have the same dialogue that Vladimir and I had started.

Now, actually, I was very scared. And I did not know if I had to smile because I belonged to the side of those who lived better. But my fear was too big to stop to contemplate my thoughts. I was going to give everything in exchange for something unknown. I felt lost within my own solitude. At the same time, I felt a silence within, almost a merciless peace. But...

What did I want to have found? I do not know, there were no benchmarks. Now more than ever I realized that there was no awareness of this absolute freedom.

Why not have put Cuba on the agenda of any given day? Perhaps we could have planned the most important elements and dogmas of our Libertad. And now that Cuba is free, entirely free, resisting the strangulation of excessive foreign monopolies in the future.. It is now that I recognize that my agenda was empty, freedom rushes in and it is all conjecture.

Really those of us on both sides have been very busy with survival and we forgot about one of the greatest sources of our joy. I believe that most of all, our lack of faith prevented us from planning for the future of the island.

What is happening isn't true maybe. The most anticipated event caught us off guard. And it is not sensible because Cubans have plenty of reasoning, interest, and courage. I proved to myself with my achievements in the United States and the other Cubans also in the different parts of the world as well as those in Cuba who resisted from their old homes. But the missing link is finally going to be found. The only difference is going to be made by an honest government, different from all the others we have suffered. This government is going to be the product of the fusion of our nobility, two exiles and one experience. At least we will not have to invent anything, the model exists, we just have to carve it, with leaders who allow us to be what we have never been, free and technologically advanced, as any country with decorum.

The excuses have run out. Times give us new systems. It is enough to contribute each of us, with the best we can give. Everyone is going to contribute to the new Cuba, even our elderly in Miami, with their pervasive radicalism. And even the musicians who emerged on that pedestal of others. We are all, inevitably, going to contribute.

So did our blacks, the ones who decided to go unnoticed, and lost sight of us by diluting themselves with the blacks of the North. These, the legitimate Cubans, the blacks of our Island are also going to see the change. And the absurd discriminations that we once showed them are going to disappear, because this is part of our best farewell to the morass of other years. The claim to have overcome all prejudice that tied us to backwardness. And if someone felt the need for prejudice, let them go to someone else's land to see what it is like.

The lesson was worth learning. The youth will also do their part, only the ones who love the country and who are the new source of innovative ideas. Those young people here and there, those who learned from the disciplines of the Americans and the others to the young people in Cuba, who already look old, we are going to give them youth and hope. Those who saw very closely the pain produced by oppression and today have sad souls and have wrinkles on their faces. Those faces that are grimaces and are still hungry. And those, those whom we lost in the battle of time, because they could not be born here, maybe we can get them back. To those who also say with honor that we kept their roots here, so that one day they come to look for them, they will see our light and the heat of our truth that they want to change their world and know the one they never had.

The closer we got, the bigger the crowd. There was a time-flavored riddle that we all wanted to decipher. I was already beginning to see the first thing that had to be done and that was to be able to unify all those people who were nothing but my own shadow. At the moment, just without perceiving it, as a dart that stuck in my heart, I started listening to the Cuban national anthem. It was already coming from very close; the voices were raised, and they were fearless. I felt a double pride in being Cuban, one who was always self-conscious, and the new one who wore the emblem of the return. Then, those who were tired and gnawed by communism sang louder than those of the "new community"; they seemed to welcome the Cuba of exile. The grimaces began to disappear, they began to smile and cry at the same time. "This is the love for Cuba," I thought. I believe that Cubans who are wandering in other parts of the world are also singing in their hearts. And everywhere, wherever there is one of our own, they are glued to the radio or the television to see what direction things are going. How blissful I was to know that for the first time in my life I was weaving my own story!

There is little time left for the New Year to be celebrated. My god. Little time, forever, to celebrate a year, a freedom, an era.

It was chilling to see that, to my left, the Cubans on my side, the newly arrived, began to take off some from their faces. And now they seemed more natural, more legitimate. It is the mask of the "North"—I thought—the repressed emotions of the best of both Cubas were premiering. It was all chilling, but genuine.

From my seat I started singing. Vladimir cried. It is good to see a man crying for his land; between sobs he sang with me. His intonation was firm and served as a guide because the Cuban National Anthem from my mouth came out slower, with the insecurity of not wanting to blaspheme its lyrics. And Vladimir looked at me, giving me confidence, as if he wanted to help me regain my identity.

As for all this, I smiled. I did not even believe it myself. I was dreaming and doubted myself. Perhaps this is our worst enemy. We inherited a doubt in our convictions which has been perpetuated over the years. Perhaps because we have never been independent, we think we cannot be, and why do I hesitate now? We have learned to wait for the solutions to reach us externally. The whole world waits from a comfortable seat in the political theater. But the actors don't need to go on stage because the actors are already here. We are the actors. Now the curtain has been lifted and there is a truth that does not require rehearsal. Again, my doubt. That doubt of ours!

I heard the anthem but more I felt the anthem, it must be true then. I feel anguish, and joy, which of the two emotions will bring the freedom of my people? Finally, the car reached its destination, and we are ready for the encounter. I do not have time to think about whether I am dreaming. After all, our delay or our uncertainty is not going to be rewarded. We must act quickly, with solid steps, because in the zoo of the international arena there are beasts waiting to scrap us.

At least there is an intrepid idea that is being made known, and that is that Cuba already has some new criteria.

CHAPTER EIGHT

Like a spring I got out of the car. I was totally transformed. People on both sides were gathering and you could barely walk. With an unknown force I began to push them away, they made me a gap, a camino. Someone from far away from the crowd shouted:

"He must be the leader".

Someone else, who knows who, replied, "Yes, he is the leader, our leader."

They began to applaud, and the applause sounded intermittent, how when the masses went mad with euphoria.

Vladimir followed me and I started hating myself. I looked like an Indian chief with his tribe on his back. "Poor people," I thought.

For now, I stopped and contemplated the joy of my people:

"A leader? A leader? I responded almost with inappropriate hatred. A leader? You still want a leader! Another leader?" —My voice was a hoarse cry of anger. They do not know who I am, where I come from, or what motives my heart holds! "No, I am not a leader. Don't you realize that I can bring you another lie even bigger than the one you have come out of? And you, those on the other side, who do you think I am? A leader, another top leader...?"

My irony was ruthless, but my message was punishing this political immaturity. We had not learned and there were only a few seconds left to capture it all.

There was silence. A grave silence that cut the soul. And there was a distant echo that took away my voice, turning it off, burying it in the air.

Vladimir surprised me. He had stood on a wall. It already looked like its own palm. His voice began to thunder. I thought I fainted, because he sounded like the waves, (always the same Malecon waves...) The words were firm, energetic, with an enigmatic cadence. He conquered us all:

"No more men who come to rule an inexperienced people. Leaders are no longer coming back because they have robbed our vitality. We are not leaders but the catalysts for reunification."

His voice also had the serenity of the waves. And I thought it was maybe that the Malecon suddenly had already learned to walk and was there next to us. Vladimir looked serene with an equanimity that shocked me. As he spoke softly, people began to sharpen their ears.

And so, this man spoke, looking at the ground, looking at the sky, as if he were talking to the distant future or with himself, as if Marti were hearing... With an indescribable loving gesture, with an immense love in his voice, he repeated for a long time the word: homeland. He said homeland and each time it sounded different. Every time it was different.

"Patria, Patria, dearest Patria..."

Now an echo came to repeat it was not taken it with it, it was left him floating free in the air and the blue sky. It was no longer just a word, but a concept that stood by the weeping people looking at their fate.

It looked like Vladimir was learning to speak or premiering his best song. He lived like his liberated world in every letter of the word...

"Patria, for you and for what you represent to me, let us hope that everyone will come, to create you fair and clean, without leaders."

I interrupted, shouting:

"That a governing group be established. That all decisions are balanced by the opinion of the whole."

So, unknowingly, we were already weaving a thousand ideas and a democracy.

Vladimir, firm as his palms, turned to the crowd. Out of his mouth came, like fire, the words of Marti, in his writing "Three Heroes"

"Freedom is the right that every man has to be honest and to think and speak without hypocrisy. There are men who live happily, even if they live without decorum. There are others who live in agony when men live without decorum around them. In the world there is a certain amount of decorum, just as there is a certain amount of light. When there are many men without decorum, there are always others who have in themselves the decorum of the many men who did not have it.".

Vladimir continued, and his voice regained strength, "those are the ones who reveal themselves with terrible force against those who rob the peoples of their decorum. With these men go thousands of men, goes to an entire village, goes the human dignity."

There was an empty space, without voices, all dressed in silence, a silence that seemed like a century, the century with more beauty that our sad history had collected. And now there were more and more people who were tightening up. He applauded softly, with respect, as if he had been Marti the one who would have conquered our hearts again. In each applause there was maturity. Every applause was an approval, a wish, a desire for prosperity and perhaps a farewell. We had learned.

And Vladimir referred to the bitter days of Castro's fall, where hatred and blood covered the greenery of the island. He also referred to the Castro rats, now in their best role as cowards. And he also mentioned the noble people who were now beginning to forgive and find the strength to create a better future. He talked a lot about forgiveness, forgiving everything. There was no room for revenge, we were all guilty at one point or another.

And I also wanted to speak in place of Marti, the apostle, the one who had brought Vladimir out of the shadows, out of Castro's inertia, and Jose Martí spoke, from my mouth:

"Freedom costs very dearly, and it is necessary, either to resign oneself to living without it, or to decide to buy it for its price"

Cuba applauded me. I was shaking. And I still had the means to say:

"There are two things that are glorious: the sun in heaven, and freedom on earth.

Vladimir moved closely and hugged me. I spoke in his language. Two men who came from different worlds were united by their apostle. I do not know who started to speak, but now Marti spoke through both of us (hopefully someone will write what is happened), and with humility our voices began to make theater, Marti's play. He started speaking and I followed him:

"Freedom is not a flag in whose shadow the victors devour the vanquished and overwhelm them with their untiring grudge: freedom is like a robust female wolf who has the sweetest of a father, love, and a mother, the richest of mothers, peace".

And so, the eternal light of Marti was released, with his message of forgiveness and strength.

That is how simple the fate of a people began to rise. The best response to all signs of tyranny had begun.

Vladimir and I were now looking at each other. We were facing each other. There was an indescribable contrast. His eyes penetrated mine, as if he wanted to make sure that my intentions, with northern features, were noble. I, for one, tried to believe in his representation and tried to gain confidence, because I knew that deep down his perspective had a certain left-wing flavor. Without a doubt, we were the direct product of our experience. But, after all, these differences would be the best balance. Besides, what could be done? We were in a political laboratory.

CHAPTER NINE

Suddenly people turned to see something new. They murmured. More murmurs... And a silence. I wanted to see, and I could not. Vladimir was wondering and asked me what it was. I did not respond. The answer came, the political prisoners arrived. They looked shipwrecked. They were náufragos. They did not walk, they crawled. That is why they were late.

They have such a hard time walking! Probably the rusty bars of their gloomy prisons opened very slowly. They were made for eternity.

They did not come alone, almost everyone came with a relative, at least a mother, maybe a friend. And those, the younger ones, the ones who could have walked faster were also coming slowly. The brightness of the sun was hurting their eyes. In their wet prisons they only had their heat. Now they lived it again. And screams of euphoria began, and it was applauded with the greatest joy. Vladimir started jumping and looking at the sky. (He believes in God.)

I understood that there had been another exile, a third exile, the worst of the three. I was still perplexed to learn that those of us on both sides here and there should have been ashamed and not complain about what we did not have. That was the final answer. Those who suffered the most made their entrance to start again as well.

I wish I could have made a very large bonfire to bury this worst memory, but we needed it. Memories will be the pillars and experience our building material. Can you learn a lot in a prison? I wondered. At the same time, freedom is appreciated in a double way.

The applause continued. The two Cubas welcome our prisoners, and how much pain we saw in those faces! Noble faces of steel. Will they shine again? Who will give them back their lost time? Those years that can no longer return and that passed while they were in their waiting capsule, waiting for death or freedom. This is the best moment, the most solemn moment of my return.

Tribute to the martyrs of the infamy of socialism. The old ones who were once young, who changed their convictions because of torture imported from Siberia. I believe that we should lower our foreheads in humility for those who suffered the most, suffer no more! I wonder if Vladimir wanted to go with me to any prison to cry for a while, to kneel and to thank God for his mercy and to thank God for his misericordia. Then we go away and close the grilles forever.

* * * * *

It took a while, a minute maybe, but enough to realize that it was already getting dark. Enough for new emotions to guide my spirit. The tropical night was opening and there in the sky the stars illuminated the victory of la patria. The sky, in its dress of light, seemed to be dancing our joy. They did not want to miss the glorious event that was transforming the Caribbean Island. I have never seen it shine so brightly. Maybe I never looked up.

The stars are going to tell the morning sun about our victory. But also, from the sky something very special was illuminated, from the sky the stars illuminated in the same way another island, Puerto Rico that also gave us shelter and entertained us with its beauty. It was the closest we had looking like the Cuba we left. That next door island that kept us always close to ours. "It looks so much like Cuba...", said some Cuban when he wanted to imagine the one that was not within reach. Puerto Rico was the only portrait that kept our memory alive. Let Puerto Rico also be illuminated, which is a piece of free Cuba...! And finally, twelve o'clock arrived: a New Year rushed in with a taste of new. There was an air of farewell and a clean era in the hearts.

It was ironic that several decades ago, on a similar night, the worst, the worst ever, a guerrilla pounced on Cuba and took it by surprise. We did not know his true intentions because he seemed honest, hidden in his youth, and promised what was necessary. After a few months, the betrayal became visible, and the people of Cuba lost their innocence. The deceptions subdued the conscience of the country and people began to abandon everything. There were no signs of hope. After so many years of waiting, begging from time to time for freedom, all confidence and vitality had run out.

On a New Year's Eve[15], a mankind's cowardice gifted power over to the worst of tyrants. And we went to the North as political refugees, and we lost our motherland. People wanting to come back. These are cycles of history perhaps. But the truth is that we gave everything for nothing. One departure, one arrival and three decades of moral and material misery.

But now there are new stars in the sky and my return is so real. I do not know if I hear the sound of the waves of the Malecon or I am carrying them with me. I think I can conquer the universe or my destiny. I see my people who are joyful again, a sad and dormant Havana that will now live in the light of these stars. And it seems as if the destruction of the city began to shine with the light of hope.

"Happy New Year, Vladimir! Viva Cuba Libre!"

---

[15] On a New Year's Eve in 1959 Fidel Castro assume military and political power as Cuba's Prime Minister

CHAPTER TEN

Morning had dawned and Havana was still asleep. A calm sun, a beginning sun, rose aloft in the clean sky. The Castro hurricane had passed, and Cuba was sleeping to the sound of the peace of a New Year.

It was the first day and people were no longer preparing to gather in the Plaza de la Revolución. This people who suffered so much were no longer going to parade tanks camouflaged with Ethiopian blood. Now the capital was to celebrate its chants of the new victory. Now the city is sleeping with the old tiredness. I think maybe the people are afraid to gather for fear of finding out that what they have experienced is not true. I think that is why I do not hear the songs and the habaneros celebrating, and there is no traffic, there is nothing. There is only silence. I have to hurry to tell these people to stop dying. And I know it is hard because you cannot build in one day the destruction of so many years. I must wake up the city. Havana has to wake up, and most of all, those who are still sleeping to forget everything.

We must hurry. There is a trial that will begin in a few hours. We are going to judge Castro. And the whole island will come. The island is going to regain its justice. I want to arrive early to greet the many reporters that will come from abroad to tell the world about our tragedy, and our victory.

I think if the press will tell the truths that for years were hidden in the Prison of the Combinado del Este[16] Or to count the tortures of Mazorra[17], hospital for the insane, where the sane ones who spoke out were kept. And if you are going to say name by name of those killed in the firing squads, and of all the thousands that the sea ripped from us

---

16 The largest prison in Cuba with maximum security in the surrounding area of Havana houses the highest concentration of political prisoners or prisoners of conscience of the island. Among them were the so-called "Planted" those who refuse to reform politically.

17 Comandante Eduardo Bernavez Ordaz also known as Mazorra is a psychiatric hospital where the Cuban government sent opponents of the regime, and many of them have lost their mental faculties due to the excesses of electroshock.

across the Straits of Florida on flimsy balsas. And, even more, if you are going to be able to narrate all the rest. And I mean not only the dead who do not live but also the living who were left dead.

You do not die only when your life is ripped away from you, but also when you conditionally give it away or take it away from a loved one. That is also how we die. So, we have all died many times. We died when we had to separate and spread throughout the world. We died when we never came back. We died when we had to beg for shelters in other lands. We died when we thought we were immune, and we talked about Cuba even louder. We died when hatred and intrigue pitted parents against siblings. We died with a friend's message, begging for medicine. Moments on the telephone calls limited by the eternal "4 minutes"[18]. We died when we learned to play the lie. We died for the fourteen thousand children sent alone as letters without senders And, even so, «half-lived», exiles have been forged made with the bronze of Maceo and the fortitude of Martí.

I wonder if other countries will participate in this tribunal. This trial is open to the world, so that it may be recognized that Marxism-Leninism as an economic and political experiment is already archived for history under: «failure». After all, what also remains of that 26 July 1953? A past that does not return and a trial that will barely begin.

Castro's trial is going to be very long, but his verdict short. All this shatters my heart, but I will be encouraged by the hum of the waves. I really want to dress up. Cuba will be present, it will look beautiful, it is its best moment. Cuba will share with me the pain of all its memories. And Havana, my dear Havana, is going to accommodate the whole island. Cuba has chosen a grand jury that goes from Pinar del Río to the East, Oriente. This trial will conclude the great nightmare that still smacks of fear.

Long live my country! Let the trial take place. This is not going to be Moncada's trial. My hands in a fist, my jaws tense... I was hating for the whole island; I knew that Castro became old, and he aged all of us.

---

18 Early years telephone calls made to the Cubans on the island by family members or friends in the United states whose duration was 4 minutes only it was controlled by the Cuban government and paid for those persons abroad.

I have to get dressed. I must arrive early to see history now judging and not absolving. And this piece of history is the one I want to know because the other one consumed my soul. The new generations will read what happened, the old ones already lived it. Will Vladimir have the list of all the accused? How many names will all the Vladimirs have? Who will carry the names of those who died distantly and fighting for other people's causes?

My God, I am exhausted by hatred! Help me, Cuba! I want to forget. I have an open wound that I want to close with you.

And in my own monologue, with my tormented mind, I feel a strange peace. I reflected on the events that have occurred...

From my window I contemplated countless flags, only Cuban flags, the legitimate ones. Without the shadow of the hammer and sickle, only that of a star.

And so, I realized that Vladimir was not with me, and I again doubted my reality and my own eloquence. Would there have been Vladimir, that man made of palm who whispers with the cadence of Marti's verses? The one who brings my Malecon with him -- where will I go to look for him? Or what other dream will I build for him and the freedom of Cuba to come? But how can I dream if I was breathing the air of the island? Maybe I haven't existed? Maybe it was just partial fantasies, part realities, parts who knows... Or is all this a product of my new horizons, and would Vladimir be the hope of all of us on any given day? I am going to go out, I want to be mingling again with all of them, the man here, who with unusual courage survived his half-death like any of those over there.

But what time is it?... There are rumors in the streets. More and more voices... Cuba is already waking up and I..., I, what do I do here?

From my window I spotted many flags. How strange it was to be free while life passed under a window... I was sure of what I saw and at the same time I did not believe it. This doubt made me crazy. I do not want to go back, Cuba... leave me here with you! Tell me that I live the truth, that I dream what I live and that I live what I dream. Look how I am crying; I do not want to go back... Please return my own dream. I do not want to dream a new one. I do not have time. Cuba's freedom is slipping through. Oh, God, understand me, I have a trial with pain of time that I must go to...

The more I thought, the more I suffered. The fear of another truth invaded everything. So, suddenly, I saw Vladimir under my window. Life stopped. I smiled at him. With a simple gesture he asked me to meet him. And so, I did... and I was perplexed contemplating Vladimir who looks like the silhouette of a palm, and I start to walk with him. I knew that Vladimir would not look back, because he was heading firmly and confidently to preside over the judgment of this history.

CHAPTER ELEVEN

I went out into the street. I breathed, lived, felt the breeze, and calmed down. I found a scruffy child, a child of ours, a Cuban child, barefooted, barefooted, and aged; he already had the premature wisdom that underdevelopment produces. He approached me. Surely, he approached all the foreigners every day. To his sad eyes, I would be one more who would come to proclaim to the world, with photos he cursed, the miseries of his people. He looked at foreigners and lived other worlds in their gestures, cameras, and clothes. Then he became a beggar or thief, without rush and without dissonance.

"I change dollars sir."

With her little hands of a beggar, he asks to the sound of the new destitution. It is so much what he knows, he has the malice that comes with surviving. I wondered why he suffered a past. Does he know that things have changed? Or is it that in his precocious omnipotence freedom is another trick?

Poor little boy, he does not know...or he knows it but do not believe it...

The pre-revolutionary beggars begged for bread, those of now have regressed in their misery, those of now ask for illicit currency because theirs does not give them even bread.

From embarrassment to embarrassment, his days grew. This child must know that the time has come to conquer his childhood. I will take him with me for him to feel the Malecon resonating differently, so that he can vibrate and recognize this moment and have its Golden Age."La Edad de Oro" I will take away his hurtful andrajos and will give him a flag.

"Come with me, immense child, to give you freedom. Come with me please and forgive us"

This child is the very symbol of what Castro promised to abolish in 1959!

I know why he seems enigmatic and sad. He is a Vladimir who did not have Marti, surely, he learned to live faster than his own time. He comes from atheistic times and has no faith and believes in nothing. His eyes were the only light that illuminated his own spirit as he is an old man and a child.

"Where did so many people go? he asks me.

I know he does know; but he does not believe it and he is looking at it. He is a sage of his time. He grew up hopeless and now he must learn to have hope.

When I looked at that child in front of me and looked at Cuba in the distance, I thought of the underdevelopment before Castro and of today's underdevelopment, that stagnancy that became more intense in recent times. In front of me, the child hurting my conscience; behind, were my people carrying the damn cross of recoil. Handing it over to our Judas will not take away its weight, but it may become lighter.

The miseries of my people hurt! The worst thing about tyrannies is that they drag what is horrendous and make it perpetual. And we vegetate, not realizing how the rest of the world turns with the inertia of new eras.

Without warning, as the rain of the tropics is intrepid, it began to rain. The fresh rain disarmed my anguish, the image of the past was diluted in my scattered fear. I looked up at the sky.

"It's just a cloud." I heard from an expert, a miniature sage, a child of yesterday.

I smiled to myself.

"We Cubans know everything!" I playfully thought.

In the midst of my reflections and the rain I didn't know when the child disappeared. Again, my fantasies, my dreams so reproached? I do not know, but his image was still there. It was simply a revelation of future times.

Looking at the past through a broken mirror was like straightening out the best image of my Cuban land.

CHAPTER TWELVE

Behind me I heard Vladimir's voice. What a joy I felt! He extended his hand, energetically, firmly, willingly. I hugged him. Now I knew that the other Cuba was also walking. Vladimir carried many old yellowish papers corroded by fear and years. They kept great secrets of horror and death. I did not want to ask, but I read in his eyes that those papers were the evidence that the world awaited. More and more people were joining us.

Now there were some cars and people with the faces of foreigners. Nobody asked anything, nobody laughed, nobody talked. There was a strange silence, unusual for the magnitude of people who followed us. I think everyone was having some concern and maybe it was the uncertainty of the purpose of all this, to believe that this meeting would be useless.

There was a lot to do in Cuba and we were banding together to hold the most painful trial in our history. After reflection, I knew that this was necessary, inevitable. An era had to be closed.

The rain began to fall again, now finer. The sky was gray, and it seemed to be crying for everything Cuba went through. And the closer we got to Revolution Square, now, changed back to Civic Square, the sky got darker. We stopped in the square, the sky began to thunder, and it was beautiful and chilling as if God were in charge of the aperture of the trial

I did not know what to do, or what to say, or whether I had to process a fair idea or preside over something. But suddenly my soul began to dictate too me minute by minute. There were no more questions or encounters with doubt. In that darkness our destiny could be seen. I realized that most of all, I was one Cuba and, more than ever, Vladimir was the other one. I already knew this, but I did not know when the others knew.

Out of some microphones came our names, Vladimir and I came out of the crowd. They began to clap; the applause was confused with the thunder and the rain. Now, we were all wet, we looked the same. Neither the skinny nor the best dressed, nor the most intelligent, nor those of New York, nor those of Miami, nor those of the prisons, we all looked the same, the Cubans hurt, soaked in the external rain and that of the heart.

* * * * *

This was not all, the black woman that I spotted from my window was arriving. She was a witness, another witness who would speak for the black people who had never emancipated themselves, the lost promise, one more. And, as a witness to another lie, the boy, shirtless, with his childhood without childhood, stood beside me. I was not surprised by his presence.

Many surprises rushed in, there was no time to assimilate them. He gave me his small, warm little hand, this child was a little palm next to me; next to us, he looked at Cuba and understood everything. As he was short, he could only look up and I was glad, because only looking up would he understand the new vision of the adults around him. And so, the people next to us and we next to them, we seemed like we were part of a play.

There in front, an audience that was also the protagonist of a drama of more than thirty years.

If there were a standing ovation, who would deserve it more, those here or there, those in front or those below? My thoughts are "still" separatist. I still have my prejudices. When will I learn?

I was glad they did not know what I was thinking about, I would have been embarrassed. I still have the errors that led to our ruin. We must stop analyzing who deserves the Cuba that awaits us the most. Anyone who wants it, even a foreigner, if he has it in the heart.

The only condition is that of not having conditions. Only the love for Cuba will be the passport to the bienvenida. No more farewells, there will only be many "see you later" and "see you soon", meetings and hugs, and more hugs. We said so many goodbyes that we exhausted them.

I want to run again and return to the Malecon, but I don't. I know that I am not perfect, but I love Cuba, I will give myself to her without conditions, always exercising my best judgment. When I stop feeling for Cuba, I will stop feeling forever. Amid my semi-drunkenness, I saw a slender woman approaching and I did not want to ask what her accusation would be, her testimony, what the historical significance would be in this orgy of truths. I did not dare ask, I feared, I doubted.

I did not want it to leave this 'scene' either again and Cuba would lose the value of her existence, whatever it was. But my intrigue was big. I continued to look at her and contemplated a different value: an inexplicable quality in the midst of so many emotions. Maybe that was it, there aren't always answers. I just know that her figure is sedative, without impulses without reactions, without prejudice perhaps. She is like an achievement, of a powerful, futurist vision. And so, I had already deciphered it, the woman I saw before is here, with the resilience and the equanimity that did not respond to momentary reactions. It was as if I was motionless, maybe I wasn't breathing, maybe I wasn't or who care if I wasn't. This was simply like a dose of calms or the necessary soothing, or soft power which would relieve hatred and volcanoes of uncontrolled forces. I think that if this land were to display the accumulated, pain, hatred and resentment, the centuries to come would be over.

No, the woman is not a witness, but a portion of common sense. Now I realize it. Only in this way, with balance, will we get Cuba out of the morass. Controlling our emotions, transforming ourselves into more efficient beings for the times ahead, just like her... And, finally, every day will be like any day of April, Cuba will re-conquer its eternal spring.

Surely the Malecon will sing its best whisper, the buzz of freedom. Poor Malecon, is old and hoarse, hoarse, like an old drunk man.

There with Vladimir, the child, the woman and I, a couple also arrived, the couple of yesterday years, the one I found in the boardwalk of Malecon. Fate separated them and each one forged a different family without each other. Sure, they learned to be happy one without the other. It seems that faith has different forms.

They had been happy yes, but in a different way. Perhaps they disguised or perished forever, but the truth is that they would no longer leave their lives now, nor would they see each other anymore, nor would they mourn that separation of so many years.

They were satisfied and happy, yes, but without each other. And now, like the others, they were coming to leave their testimony.

I imagined how sad their reunion would have been. Maybe there was inertia in their emotions, maybe a closing kiss. However, there was certainly a very acute pain. Surely this was nothing more than the reality of a present that had broken a young dream of love.

When I reflect, in all the damage that tyrannies cause to their peoples, there is a lot of talk about the parents who lost their children, but there are other martyrs as well, because they lost children they did not even have.

The couple of yesteryear is now in a hurry, they want justice too, that is why they are here. An event with double pain, pain of banishment from broken futures. They had a lot to reproach the regime for, but they have to forgive history, or fate. A political event separated them; now another, with its impressive impact, united them.

Surely it hurts that a government had played with a love that now only tasted like revenge. Someone decided for them, the same one who decided for everyone else. It seemed that they were brave, but they are crying inside.

CHAPTER THIRTEEN

Amid my entangled thoughts and confused joy, I was frightened, I felt dread, hatred, revenge, and I had to look at the woman to remember my best posture and to calm down. I did not get to glance Castro as he arrived, but his energy stirred me up. I thought if it was sensible or necessary to have this trial and to this I hesitated again. Then I looked to calm myself with the hand of the child and I squeezed it trembling, I gazed at Vladimir, I looked again at the woman, and all this calmed me down. Suddenly I noticed that the boy's face was really that of Vladimir when he was a boy. I looked for Vladimir's face and there were two, I got it, two in one and one in two. The future, the past and the present, which was me. All square, firm and immense, like our Cubans palms. Fearless, with no doubts, with all Marti's hopes. Here all of us, giving energy to this important process, were waiting for the last encounter with deception. Already calm, in a unique way, I learned that in Cuba another generation of mambises (had formed, with the necessary fortitude to face the reconstruction that was expected at the end of the trial.

But, once and for all, what are we doing? What wound, my God, are we opening? And it was the couple of yesterday that I saw in the Malecon at first and now here with their pain mixed in their ashes of yesterday, who injected courage in us to realize our goal: we were reproaching, judging, and condemning all our dead and all the living who live dead...

*****

Yes, to move on. Everyone has different reasons to be here. Identical reasons, at least similar. And so, I spot an old man who was clumsily heading toward me. He walked so slowly that it seemed like all his accumulated years were hurting him. Out of respect no one interceded him. His audacity was striking. He stood alone. Now that he was very close, he extended his trembling, and wrinkled hand. He was sobbing, and I wanted to cry too. I was drowned by grief looking at this man. Poor old man, he suffered. He reached my hand and gave me a piece of rolled up paper and said very softly:

"My son left it to me. This is my debt, sir. "I wanted to hold him, but he turned around and left, carrying his old age, and got lost in the multitude .

The paper he left was a letter, which I dared to read:

"Dad, I want to say goodbye. I will no longer return home; I will be crossing the gulf in search of freedom. I am a good son, daddy, sorry for the pain I am causing you, but I am vegetating in my twenties. I cannot do it anymore! If I make it, I will send for you. I trust in this, but if the sea were to take me, even after I died, I will always love you.

Your son Juan."

I do know how long my eyes were contemplating this piece of evidence. Now I squeezed the letter and put it next to my heart.

It was, my God, the same pain that my father felt when I left; only then I lived, and my father was consumed by the waiting and all the nostalgia he felt. Now... Now that I had come back to find, he is no longer here, but only his bones.

And to think that, that one day I saw him, I left and just like that it was the last day for the of rest of my life.

Who pays for these things? These are eternal damages... this is my debt... But...will we recover? We must!

The years have given us conformity and will give us even more. You have to have courage. Here everything happens quickly, in retrospect, mercilessly. That is why we must forgive, because we are running out of time.

And, and where, where the old man go?

Surely, he went to die peacefully knowing his debt is here, his debt is mine now.

"I am your other son.".

* * * * *

I did not want to give this letter to Vladimir. The testimonies he carried were many. They were too heavy. So hurtful. I just carried this letter and my whole life.

Then I looked out front. I saw everyone thirsty for guidance and direction.

There was a fear in their hearts, a new fear, a fear with a certain logic. They did not want a leader, but a guide. I looked at the everybody and I saw the fear there waiting, the fear of what I learned, the fear of experience.

What to do to never fall again into the same tragedy?

Never! Never! The first thing would be to collect this story and to store it in a place that is very accessible to those who tend to forget. And the second, the third and the fourth. With memory and unity, we will move forward.

I knew that, more than a trial and a judgment, there was a longing for the future and all that was coming.

I looked at the group that was made in the United States and I hoped that they brought, for the beginning, certain capitalist democratic knowledge. I imagined my American experiences hand in hand with everyone's experiences, trying to alleviate the 'child' representing our underdevelopment. With the equanimity acquired and the help of the hundreds of Vladimirs, the debts of the old ones paid off and the prisons open, we will finally be able to integrate ourselves into the planet. No more wandering revolutions. The guerrilla spirit is taken away by the equanimity of the woman.

The couple with their past is here. Quite a start for them. And so, we all leave the old time to create our new time, our best time. My soul is full! Discipline is the hope. The achievements are almost beginning. There is so much energy that this town brings, that we will make up for each lost year, five better!

There are many who are not here now and say they are in Cuba. They are crying in the Malecon, or painting a façade, or kneeling in front of a Virgin... or breathing in some corner of the East, or Matanzas, or Camaguey. No matter, we are all seeing it! Each one is bringing his or her best start. I bring a smile, a form, a way, a process.

That is how I did. That is how I was made. I come made from the North. I looked in the distance and imagined one flag, the other, the flag of many stars, the flag of power, the great American flag! And I could still cry again: Thank you for everything! I know I am not ungrateful, but I can't continue to be divided. I infinitely thank you for your stars. Each of them illuminated me in exile. And they made me who I am today, maybe a better entity... I know you get it. Oh, God, this flag always understands.

I lowered my forehead with respect, with humility, and from my hands sprouted a wrinkled and broken flag: the Cuban flag. With my identity more composed, with joy and with some sorrow, with the honesty of a new man, I exclaimed:

"This flag, look at it everybody, look at it everyone, please look at it, you all! This one needs me more. It is also mine and it is ripped, the Cuban one, the one with one star.

CHAPTER FOURTEEN

When I woke up in my Miami bed, my clean, comfortable bed, from my commercial and frivolous world, I knew that what I experienced had only been the product of strange, or elevated stages perhaps- the world of my dreams. Now, all torn up inside, I said goodbye to the best part of me. I wanted to integrate myself into the daily routine. As it was difficult, I became a sad and gloomy man. I felt the bitterness of my own deception and could do nothing because my enemy was myself.

Wandering and rambling, I lived tired for many days. I was disappointed. Everything was the same around me. All over again the same thing, freedom fell asleep, vanished in my hands, it got trapped as a prey of my own dream.

Perhaps, if he, Vladimir had woken up next to me, the entire island would also have woken up.

For those who seemed to hear me, I had the courage to explain myself. They did not understand me entirely, they did not make fun of me either, they did not look at me. It made no impact. Always the same inertia, that's how they reacted, those in the North. The magnitude was mine alone. My world still is not being perceived. Where will I go with my dreams? My great and stormy dreams of freedom!

Everything bothered me, the people, the contrasts, what an agony. Where to escape? Where to recreate the noble image of Vladimir, the only hope of a redeemed people? And so, the days, months all passed and went. And many ones dawned, and my Vladimir never again returned. Neither Vladimir, nor the Malecon, nor its breeze, nor its glory... All that was left was just feeding my guilt.

Wasn't all that even a premonition? I was consumed by the weariness. I was reluctant to give up something so timely. Perhaps reality is that when you are sleeping all appears and disappears and doesn't return anymore. The rest, the rest is what remains, just a burden. With my dream I could feel freedom, and freedom had space, time, and dimensions. And it was the future, and it was Marti, and we were all meeting and forgiving each other.

I was all confused, another day, one more boring day, but then suddenly it became important. I was starting to dress like when you do not want to go anywhere. I heard on the television coming from the next room the "fall of Castro." Like a spring it put me on alert. I did not know more until I woke up in a hospital. Then a voice whispered to me:

"It's true!"

I was afraid that it wasn't. I was afraid that it was!

Fidel Castro had fallen! It was true, historical, unique. I learned that there is a similarity between the truth, dreams, reality, and madness. In these scenes only the dynamics change.

For this new drama I was preparing myself, not to hurt myself. And there, in my bed, all disillusioned and tired, I waited ready for anything. My wife does not lie. I thought. Will Vladimir be there again? The one who judged me at first as a mercenary for buying my freedom at a discount in a war?

My wife was already talking about Vladimir, she already knew the partner in my dreams. Maybe she doesn't want to tell me the truth, so I don't hurt myself.

I wonder if she feels sorry for me, or she wants me well.

"What do I have doctor? Que mas dá…" I have also learned to know it all.

Diagnosis: EXILE.

Epilogue

"In the magic of a dream Cuba was free already." By Octavio R. Costa 1991

The dream has been used as a skillful artifice to produce a literary work. Just remember Quevedo's famous book. Ileana González Monserrat, up to now literary unknown, has utilized to this procedure. These pages of Havana, 1995 are enough to be definitively consecrated as one of our brightest and most solid intellectual contributors within of our current youth.

Manolo Salvat, with his usual kindness, gave me a copy. At that time, I could not face reading it no matter how much I was attracted by the enigmatic title on a simple, beautiful, and original cover. And when the book was still unread, without me losing sight of it, I was introduced to Ileana at in a recital by Zenaida Manfugás and I was told she was the author of the book Havana 1995.

It was a pleasant surprise to learn that she was a neighbor in Los Angeles. In this first and only vision I had of her I found her young, distinguished, and beautiful. Unfortunately, we could not speak. But the meeting served to get me immediately into the eighty pages of this dream of hers that took her to Havana on New Year's Eve 1996.

The first thing to say is that Ileana knows how to write. A prose that fulfills that golden law that Azorín- Jose Augusto Trinidad, the Spanish novelist and literary critic of the 1890's enunciated and that is very simple: "to say things one after another and not one within another". And so, she does .

She writes on a dream plane with the way all dreams have of being of fragmentary, illogical, and gelatinous. There is no incoherence because it doesn't appear in the magical adventure that Ileana's thoughts while she slept, or the protagonist slept.

We must insist on the quality of the prose of this writer who is now revealed to us because she exhibits unsealed values. I totally do not know her literary background. I know nothing about the rest of her writings. And it is because of this lack of familiarity that I react with such surprise to these pages of so much poetic breath, and that they have delighted me so much.

Ileana masters the short sentence. Her words offer very precious edges despite the inconsistent raw material she uses to construct the fiction that serves to expose her thoughts in Cuba.

The protagonist enters the dream and finds himself in Havana, and in the Malecon. A large sign reveals that he is there on the eve of a new year, that of 1996, and from this message he senses that Cuba is already free and that the date favors the joyful celebration that has not been had for so many years.

As in every dream he suddenly changes places, he is in front of a car from 1951. He goes to the driver. They are soon identified, overcoming all distances. The one who narrates the dreamlike adventure is a Cuban who has returned to the island from the United States. His name is Juan, but they call him John. The other, who, as he himself says, did not have the alternative of his interlocutor, has always lived on the island. He is Vladimir.

The name reveals everything. And on a journey through Havana that Vladimir gives to the one who has been absent, Juan is connected to the city that he left long ago, the author began with the revealing stories of each of them so different, but in which Ileana sees a lot of commonalities .

Vladimir is a Cuban who has suffered the falsification that communism has imposed on his true personality. And John has had to immerse himself in American society and identify with its culture. Apparently, he is an accomplished man, but at the cost of his most endearing Cuban values.

Neither is what they would have been if they had lived in a Cuban republic, an historical reality that had nothing to do with their making.

The author lives a succession of moving scenes that she traces with the most realistic plasticity and that she seasons with the sharpest comments. All of them refer to the return of the exiled Cubans with the additional apparition of the free prisoners. It is the inexorable reunion of two peoples who for three long decades have lived within very different conditions though their essences are the same. And already before the excitement of the trial that the people will hold, the prisoner who has been prosecutor and executioner, abruptly evaporates because Ileana wakes up the protagonist and the dream is broken.

Now that it is presumed that the communist regime is close to being trampled and that the Cuban in Cuba is so different than the Cuban exile, we must read these revealing pages, so literally beautiful and so shockingly Cuban. We all learn a lot from the magical dream of this young woman who now surprises us with a volume that cannot be ignored. It will prepare the mood and attitude for the date.

Diario Las Américas, August 21, 1991

The author in the Berlin Wall, 1991

F

The author in Versailles Restaurant, Miami July 11, 2021. mcusa photo.

www.ingramcontent.com/pod-product-compliance
Lightning Source LLC
Chambersburg PA
CBHW020603030426
42337CB00013B/1182